Animals in Cold Countries

Written by Diana Bentley
and Dee Reid

This is a penguin.
Penguins have big beaks.
They like to eat fish.

This penguin jumped off the ice and into the water.

This is a seal.
Seals have big flippers.
They go into the sea
to find fish to eat.

Seals like to sleep on the ice.

This is a walrus.
Walruses have big tusks.
They eat fish, but some big
walruses will eat seals too.

Walruses like to sleep in the sun.

This is a polar bear.
Polar bears have big paws.
They like to eat seals, but they
will eat fish too.

Polar bears like to play in the snow.

This is a killer whale.
A killer whale will
find penguins and
seals to eat.

A killer whale can eat a walrus.
Could a killer whale eat a
polar bear?

Some killer whales could!